REAL NEWS

REAL NEWS

new and collected poems by
Stacie Smith

Shanti Arts Publishing
Brunswick, Maine

REAL NEWS
New and Collected Poems

Copyright © 2019 Stacie Smith

All Rights Reserved
No part of this book may be used or reproduced in any manner whatsoever without the written permission of the publisher.

Published by Shanti Arts Publishing
Interior and cover design by
Shanti Arts Designs

Shanti Arts LLC
193 Hillside Road
Brunswick, Maine 04011
shantiarts.com

Cover image by Stacie Smith, *Rosie and the Farm Cats*, 1980s. Used with permission.

Printed in the United States of America

ISBN: 978-1-947067-64-6 (softcover)

Library of Congress Control Number: 2019940591

for Sidney and Amedee

"We do not have to live as if we are alone."

— Wendell Berry
"It All Turns on Affection"
Jefferson Lecture 2012

CONTENTS

I. REAL NEWS

WHO ASKS TO BE BORN?	14
MIRROR BY THE DOOR	15
FLAME	16
AND THEN WE'RE NOT	17
NEWS WORTH BREAKING	18
REAL NEWS	19
WEAPON OF CHOICE	20
FOR SYRIA	22
FULL CIRCLE	23
AGAIN	24
PLAYA SERIES VIII	25
PLAYA SERIES IX	26
WORLD NEWS	28

II. WHAT THE CROW KNOWS

PLAYA SERIES I	30
UP	31
WHAT THE CROW KNOWS	32
ILLAHE II	33
ILLAHE III	34
TOO SACRED TO SAY	35
CREDO	36
HEADWATERS	37
YARD WORK	38
ASK	39
KIAHANIE	40
PERSIEDES	41
DONNA'S PROMPTS SERIES I: SOUL GEOLOGY	42
RIDGELINE TRAIL	43

(continued)

III. NOTHING IS WRONG

- PLAYA SERIES VII ... 46
- HIGH TIME ... 47
- HOW ELSE COULD HUNGER ... 48
- MOUNT UNION CEMETERY ... 49
- MONDAY ... 50
- U-STOR ... 51
- PLAYA SERIES III ... 52
- ARI'S GIFT ... 53
- WHAT ELSE I CAN DO ... 54
- DEPARTURE ... 55
- OLD GROWTH ... 56
- BURIAL ... 57
- LAST WILL ... 58
- NOTHING IS WRONG ... 59
- THE COLOR OF SNOW ... 60
- JANUARY ... 61
- STONEHOUSE ... 62

IV. WHATEVER IT IS

- ANOTHER TAKE ... 66
- QUIET ROOM ... 67
- TWO HEARTS COLLIDE ... 68
- HALF MOON ... 69
- WHATEVER IT IS ... 70
- EMPTY PAGE ... 71
- LETTER FROM SEA LEVEL TO MY FAMILY ... 72
- EMILY'S POEMS ... 73
- NOTHING LEFT TO SELL ... 74
- ONE FOR THE PREY ... 75
- DONNA'S PROMPTS SERIES XIV: CRYING MOUNTAIN ... 76
- THE LETTER ... 77
- NEXT ... 78
- WHO CARES IF THE WORLD ENDS? ... 79

ACKNOWLEDGMENTS

The author expresses thanks to the editors of the following publications in which these poems first appeared:

Open Burning: "Another Take," "Two Hearts Collide," "Letter From Sea Level To My Family," "Ari's Gift," "Last Will," "Stonehouse," "Playa Series I," "Too Sacred To Say (Cougar Creek Series XXXVI)," "World News"

Interlace: "Half Moon"

Jefferson Monthly: "Playa Series I," "Playa Series VIII"

I.
REAL
NEWS

WHO ASKS TO BE BORN?

A poem does,
and when it's ready
it starts pushing
on the walls
of its word-womb.
>Nothing can stop it
>once it starts.
>It needs help
>along the way
>of course.

For starters
a vessel, a seed,
good luck
and a long spell
in darkness,
and after
its hard labor,
willing hands
to receive it.

MIRROR BY THE DOOR

>I've had it with the human news.
>It's getting old.

>I've had it with the human race.
>Can I resign?

>I want to flee this ruined house
>and find a kinder, gentler place.

I check the mirror by the door
and see my very human face.

FLAME

Outpaced again
by the doers of deeds
headline makers
and record breakers

I sit here spellbound
by a single candle flame
more newsworthy than the news
for its vital implications:

shadows are caused
by light

wick and wax vanish
as they burn

aimed at a flame, human breath
makes shadows dance

AND THEN WE'RE NOT
Cougar Creek Series XXXIX

Detoxing from the human news
is hard — the rush that comes from thinking
that the world's about to end, and then it's not
and then it is again — it's hard to quit.

Can't get enough of pundits telling me
exactly what it means when so-and-so
says such-and-such: we're all about to die
— and then we're not.

I tell myself to try to chill
and pray for peace but then
my mind's eye lines my enemies
against a wall and blows them down!

Could I really handle peace?
Addicted to the to and fro, the lurch
from high to low and back again —
could I handle peace?

I came to this green place today
to listen to the downhill stream.
    The breaking news it sings to me is
    Life is but a dream

NEWS WORTH BREAKING
Cougar Creek Series LII

Lately I've been tuning out the human news
and turning toward the deep dark woods
where what is real can drink its fill
of winter's pristine silence.
How did I go for so long without it?

Never mind. Here I am, now,
beside the spawning stream.
If I stand still long enough
perhaps I'll see the Coho surge
upstream to spawn and die.

This is news worth breaking.
But who would buy it?
        The salamander? The snail?
        The spawning stream itself,
        spilling its way downhill?

REAL NEWS

    Starting a fire
    with today's news
    I lit a match,
    watched headlines
     go up in smoke.
They all said
the same thing:
"WE BETTER
GROW UP FAST!"

    But the real news is:
    we're motes of stardust
    floating in the dark
    and groundless,
    adrift with our fears.
Here's the headline
I would write:
"RELAX! IT'S ONLY
SMOKE AND MIRRORS!"

WEAPON OF CHOICE

In this epoch of gunfire
my weapon of choice

is a poem, a song,
a good laugh.

> Call me crazy,
> but I do see a way
>
> away from this madness.
> It has a name I'm just
>
> learning to say.

Is it a rhyme?

A melody?
A punchline?

I'm not sure just yet
but I do know

there's a lightness to it,
a ferocity,

a dark sorrow tinged
with the radiance

of joy and grief.
    Most of my days

        are full of wandering
        and wondering.

One thing I know
is this —

there's a golden thread
that glimmers in and out of sight.

        It sometimes whispers to me
        befriend the night.

FOR SYRIA

In my garden
sunflowers lean ground-ward,
the weight of their mighty heads
pulling them down,
each seed a universe of nourishment
for any creature with wings.

News from Damascus
weighs me down
as I step into this leafy marketplace.
What can I do but witness
and proclaim: here various species
vie peacefully for what sustains.

> The finch, the bee, the chickadee,
> even the raucous jay
> all share the wealth.
> Why make war?
> We all seek the same nectar,
> seek the same seed.

FULL CIRCINE
— on returning to my hometown

I got back just in time
to see the hawthorn berries
swell and ripen on the flanks
of Spencer Butte, and smell
the pine and fir and cottonwood.

Meanwhile the human news is wild —
a person could get swallowed
if they took it for the gospel truth.
War is older than these hills —
why call it "news"?

Born in the shadow
of a mushroom cloud,
I grew to be addicted to
the possibility of something new.
War is why I pray the way I do.

AGAIN

I woke up grateful for this day
with bread and poems in it.
Oh, I know the news is bad
and certain men behave
as if they own the world
but evidence abounds
that everyone who's born
will someday lose it all

and kindness rises
every morning with the sun and
goes to work to bake the bread
while in another part of town
a poet notices the slant of light
and putting pen to page
begins again to try
to set things right.

PLAYA SERIES VIII
— after a drive up the Chewaukan River

Who knew
that paradise
was so alive and well?

>Oh, perilous times
>for sure —
>it's all over the news.

But I say: even under
perilous threat,
glory is glory

and if I can't
love the broken day
precisely as it is

>how real is hope
>for better days
>to come?

PLAYA SERIES IX

I've heard it said
        that when a butterfly
        deep in the Amazon
        unfurls then flaps its wings,
        somewhere in Iowa
        or Kazakstan a curtain
        flutters in that breeze

and when I sneeze
        a little tremor ripples
        out across the globe
        and in some kitchen
        halfway round the world
        a woman hears her dishes
        rattle in the sink.

It's called, I think,
the web of life,
but busy as you are
you may not yet
have heard this
liberating news.

I want you to!
And there is nothing
I would rather do
than send this urgent word
that we are one. It's true.
It's true.

WORLD NEWS

Over there
strange happenings.
Over here
stranger yet.

Meanwhile the iris,
regal and tall
shares a raku vase
with bright lupin.

An amber candle burns.
Smoke from sweet incense
rises and dissipates
reminding me:

opinions about the world
are not the world.

II. WHAT THE CROW KNOWS

PLAYA SERIES I

A silence
that I didn't even
know I craved
came to my door
and opened it.
First the Redwings
next the Sandhill Cranes
the Meadowlarks
the Crows.
There's something
they all know
that can't be said.
I'm here
to study *that*.

UP
Cougar Creek Series XXXVIII

Steep climb
up and up
through foxglove
sword fern
salmonberry.
Up and over
fallen cedar
to a place
feels like
no one has
ever been
— but no —
I hear
the tiny wren
insist
she got here
first!

WHAT THE CROW KNOWS

That glossy architect, the crow,
with its dark wings and raucous cry,
knows how form serves function.
Watch it build a cradle that can shift
and never shatter even when the branches
bend and tremble in a summer storm.
Watch it as it makes a place of safety
where its young can grow, then fledge,
then fly away.

The crow knows things I'll never know,
but I have eyes to witness what it does
and I can try to tell about the way
its body glistens like obsidian
and how its eye is fiery like the sun.
I can try to tell about the marvels that I see.
A wild intelligence informs the day
and everything within its ken,
including you and me.

ILLAHE II

At Illahe I heard the sound
of crows' wings rowing through fog.
In the maple overhead
clouds of small green birds
clamored for grubs.
The river itself reflected
the color of sky and
carried the colors of stone
and willow and fir
toward the sea through places
that have no human name.

ILLAHE III

Fishing without a pole
using the moment for bait
    I'm angling for words
    to approximate this day.

Two different kinds
of cricket song —
    the low slow pulsing
    and the high trilling one —

the snide call of the Stellar's Jay
the moist black grove of mushrooms
    pushing through the forest floor
    that raucous cry of Crow.

Those veins of serpentine
the color of rust and night
    that flash of silver
    where the heron spears its prey

the rippled wake and shadow
of the one that got away . . .

TOO SACRED TO SAY
Cougar Creek Series XXXVI

some things feel
too sacred to say
but i'll try anyway:
those bodies
undulating
dark and wild
pulled upstream
by lust and memory
how must it feel
to be driven
by such certainty?
when i first saw
coho spawn
in cougar creek
i didn't believe
my eyes.
fearful awe
came over me.
that vision altered me
stopped my heart
my breath
repaired my sight
recalibrated
— utterly —
my sense
of what is right

CREDO

My religion is the salmonberry
and the thrush, the lichen
and the downhill stream.

> Don't get me wrong —
> I know those holy guys
> meant well — but still

I pray instead to nettle and to fern.
I praise the salamander and the wind,
and I believe the crow.

HEADWATERS

These days I live beside
a tiny creek that flows
into a larger stream
that flows into a concrete
channel running all the way
through town with its effluvia,
then west toward a reservoir
that used to be a lake.

These days I look around
and wonder why we shouldn't
drown in our own soup.
Who knows? It just might be
delicious! Ask the Wolf,
the Hartebeest, the Golden Toad,
or that amazing flightless bird,
the Dodo, how it tastes
to be extinct.

YARD WORK

A wasp the size
of my fingernail
nailed me today.
My arm ballooned
and reddened and
as the swelling spread
I thought that I might die
and so I sat and breathed
and said and said and said
a deity's name.

There was no one else
around to rescue me.
Well, I survived.
But did that wasp?
I wonder if it lived
to sting another day.
I couldn't say.
       I only know
       it taught me
       how to pray.

ASK

Have you noticed how,
in silence, the inner ear
can hear the heart-beat
and the drum of blood
pushing into and through
the belly of the mind
with its hunger to see
and feel and hear
and know?

How did it happen,
this being born as "I",
as eye? Don't ask me!
Ask the red-tail hawk.
Ask its prey — what's left of it —
white feathers floating down,
blood on the beak, the talon,
the wing, the memory of flight.

KIAHANIE
    — for Amedee and Donna

A girl who thought she knew it all
has died, and in her place
       a speechless woman sits and watches
          as the Middle Fork Willamette passes by.

An osprey lands and perches high up
in a Douglas Fir across the waterway.
       The raptor and the woman
       look each other in the eye.

Eventually the osprey flies downstream
and in the shadow of a mossy yew
       the woman wonders how to stay alive
       not knowing what the osprey knows.

PERSIEDES
  — for Mary Jane

The Persied showers fall tonight.
Meanwhile my neighbor's aged mother

starts her fiery arc away from us
and everything she's ever known.

Her ninety-year trajectory
shines bright from here to there

out where the Persieds rain down
tiny bits of cosmic dust

igniting as they hit
Earth's atmosphere.

I wonder — if it's gravity
that makes the Persieds burn

and burning, glow,
    what force extinguishes a life

        then lets it go?

DONNA'S PROMPTS SERIES I

prolonged exposure/crystalline/
cleanse/woven/relent

SOUL GEOLOGY

Prolonged exposure to cold or heat
or pressure or time
or all of these at once
can create ice or diamonds or dust
or mysterious crystalline forms.

Fire can cleanse or kill.
If the various pressures relent,
the soul, if not held in place
by the woven strands of love and innocence
can shatter or melt, rise or fall.

RIDGELINE TRAIL

Caught between the conflagration and the hurricane
I sit and contemplate the odds of
      getting out of here alive.
I'm told and I believe that life is but a dream
      but still —
this dream includes my children and the crickets
and the woodlands and the downhill stream.

My father always told me "Keep an even keel!"
and oh I try but still — at times like this
it's hard to keep the boat from rocking
and I can't pretend this nightmare isn't real.

It seems there's nothing left to burn or drown
or blow away and so I may as well seek refuge
on the Ridgeline Trail — what's left of it — and
thank the ground for always being there
and ask forgiveness of the human race.

End times or the beginning of a brand-new day?
Is there a difference?
Either way, I witness evidence
at every step along the trail;
a wild intelligence prevails —
just look — Fireweed, Thistle, Queen Anne's lace.

III.
NOTHING IS WRONG

PLAYA SERIES VII

Massive body of stone
       topped with snow to the
       west
       between me and home.

East of Winter Rim this place
       of last resort on the shore
       of an ephemeral lake.

Now I remember why I came —
       to hear and see
       the Sandhill Cranes

and sit with what my teacher
said —
       "Your job is to find what the
       world
       is trying to be."*

*from "Vocation" by William Stafford

HIGH TIME

I wanted to settle down.
My heart was set on it
but reality intervened.
It had other plans for me —
more time on the road.

I thought it was prudent
to hand over the keys
but these itchy feet
got the best of me
like they always do.

I thought it was high time
to hang up my spurs,
but then along came
another dream-horse
to carry me away.

HOW ELSE COULD HUNGER

Until now I've been
looking at maps
to find my way
when all along,
who knew?
It's been wisdom
keeping me lost
for so long!
How else
could hunger
have driven me
to your door?

MOUNT UNION CEMETERY
— Philomath, Oregon

It's not a Mount by any stretch
but that's what they named it,
this rise of land on the edge
of my mother's hometown.
Her mother's mother is buried here,
and other kin I never met 'til now.
There's really nothing I can do
but kiss the hallowed ground.
Too late for questions that
I didn't know enough to ask.

West of here by fifty miles or so
the Pacific Ocean rolls and roils
while east of here a fertile valley
stretches all the way to mountains
many times the height of where
my forbears now lie unified with soil.
Standing here and bound like them
by land, I ask my matrilineal ghosts
to show me how to live, remind me
who — and what — I truly am.

MONDAY

While hanging out the wash
I notice my strong eye seeing
the flap and billow of damp,
functional color,
each clothespin a good deed.
>Now the pajamas will dry,
>the towels will bleach and sweeten
>in the wind, each wooden pin
>an alleluia in the August sun.

My weak eye, mind's eye,
sees something else.
Here, no usefulness,
no object but delight exists,
nothing linear or fixed
on which to clip the things
I think I need.
>And when my two eyes focus
>to function as one
>I see the day as it is,
>shining in the washday sun.

U-STOR

If I should die before
I circle back around
to where I've parked the stuff
I've tried and tried to minimize
on my way out the door
my sons can deal with
all the artifacts my time
on Earth has spawned:
the rocking chair, the lamp,
the bowl and spoon, the scroll,
the vase, the candlestick and drum,
the book and pen, the table
and the stool, the rugs,
the jugs, the pots and pans —
so much detritus — random bits
of evidence that in my younger days
I had ambition and a plan.
But now as I prepare to hit the road
I feel my spirit lift a little
as it starts a journey of its own
away from things and even from
the very place that I've called home,
and with thanks to U-STOR
I begin my weightless way
toward the great Unload.

PLAYA SERIES III

I came with a plan
        but the wind off the ridge
        undid it.

That project proposal —
        the dog in my dream
        ate it.

I thought I knew
        what I needed to know,
        put my ducks on a list

in a row
        but the meadowlarks
        deleted it.

ARI'S GIFT

My grandson found
the perfect stick.
He handed it to me and said
"Just point this magic wand.
Say OCCULUM REPARO!
It can transform things
or make them disappear!"

I keep that wand at hand
and through the day
I point it at the murky sky
and west toward the sea.
OCCULUM REPARO!
I point it at the thirsty ground
and then, at me.

WHAT ELSE I CAN DO

Now that I'm invisible
and no one notices what I do,
I can get away with anything.
From behind veils
of grey transparency
I can commit acts
of benign sabotage
like rocking the boat,
speaking out of turn,
and taking no for an answer.

Here's what else I can do
while no one sees:
look a gift horse in the mouth,
play with matches and fire,
take candy from strangers
and count my chickens
before they hatch.
I can stay up all night
writing poems by the light
of a candle burning at both ends.

DEPARTURE

Approaching the runway
the jet in my dream
revved and roared,
rolled faster and faster
then surged and lifted
as its landing gear
folded into place.
Then it banked smoothly
up and over the town
I once called home.
When finally fully aloft
I looked down
at what had been —
a dream within a dream.

No one told me
it would be like this —
departure, I mean —
so easy, so swift,
so out of this world.
I don't remember
booking this trip
but here I am,
miles high, at the mercy
of mystery, winging it,
all things once familiar
now dovetailing
dream into dream
into dream.

OLD GROWTH

Headed for the great collapse
my body took a detour suddenly
      and found itself among the pine,
      the fir, the cedar and the oak.

Their silence stopped me in my tracks
and now I don't know where to go
      but in and down the way these giants do,
      by standing still and taking root.

BURIAL

Today I decided my burial.
It will be here where I've lived so long.
It will be in a pine or cedar box
or maybe just me not wrapped
in any shroud but me
just skin to skin with earth.
I saw how old Rosie made the sod rich
as she became sod, pushing up
the tallest grasses on the hill,
her vigorous Bloodhound decay
causing wildflowers.

LAST WILL

Today I finally wrote my will!
I feel so good to know
my vast estate will go
in equal parts to those I love:

> those bits of rope and string,
> the hats, the gloves,
> those journals that I meant to burn.
> those jars of nails and screws,
>
> the bristle brush, the spoons,
> the mining shares whose value
> plunged to zero long ago,
> this pencil and those pens.
>
> The books, the tools,
> the candlestick and drum,
> the aloe and the vase,
> perhaps a memory of my face,
>
> the trowel and the hoe,
> the appetite to see and know,
> the love I wanted to convey,
> the many words I meant to say.
>
> The love I wanted to convey,
> The many words I meant to say.

NOTHING IS WRONG
— Otter Rock, Oregon

Nothing is wrong —
snowfall in summer
a crack in a cup
lost maps, stolen keys
broken hearts —
nothing is wrong.

The storm moves in
loud and dark
like a gang of crows
and nothing is wrong.
      Everything ages and breaks
      and nothing is wrong.

THE COLOR OF SNOW
— for Carolyn

It's only a prayer,
        this feeling that starts
        at the break of day.
        Birds head south
        in dark flocks
        or in pairs or alone,
        stranding us here
        bereft of their songs
        while the grey settles in
        and the prayer hurts all day
        like a bruise on a bone.
        I only know what I see —
        leaves the color of blood
        blanket the ground.
        Breath-clouds
        the color of snow
        hover, then disappear.

JANUARY

Winter shrouds the morning
but my thoughts fly to the tropics.
My body, vessel of the mind,
craves a kinder season —
warm wind and mangoes,
a bright blue-green sea
and spectacular noisy birds.

But here I am, thoughts and all,
snowbound, awaiting the thaw.
Sheathed in ice and immobilized,
our town has become a place
of treacherous crystalline beauty.
Eventually this pall will lift.
Meanwhile my mind's eye dances.

STONEHOUSE

Eager to leave
      but not sure where to go

I sit and watch steam rise
      from my cup of China tea —

how it billows, spreads
      and dissipates —

this yearning
      is like that.

Old Stonehouse wrote
      his mountain poems

from a hermit's perch
      watching "snowflakes swirl

above a glowing stove."*
      How would it be

*from *The Mountain Poems of Stonehouse*, translated by Red Pine

to live above the fray
        and never need or want

to go away?
        I may never know —

this yen for leaving
        follows me no matter

where I go and so
        I may as well just stay

and drink my tea
        and watch the steam

rise from the cup
        and let this yearning

fill me up.

IV. WHATEVER IT IS

ANOTHER TAKE
 — on global warming

Let's pretend that God's in charge —
let's say She's cranking up the heat because
She wants us done to sweet perfection
like my mother's rhubarb pie.

Let's say that there's a plan we just don't see —
a cosmic picnic in a sacred grove
where we're the honored guests
served up by God as just desserts.

Or let's look at it another way —
we're cooked, and there is nothing left to do
but feed the poor and stop the war
and keep on loving fiercely what remains.

QUIET ROOM

Where there was certainty
now there's a quiet room.
My friends have moved out
closing the door behind them

heading for the border
between night and day
where refugees fill the camps
to overflowing.

Should I follow
or should I stay behind
in this new terrain,
this wilderness of Don't Know?

> East of here is a deep cave
> where silence rings like a bell.
> In that place, legend says,
> war and peace are lovers.

TWO HEARTS COLLIDE

What's the worst that can happen
when two hearts collide?

> Well, the world stops of course,
> then by fits and starts

> begins to spin again
> though with a strange new tilt,

> its axis having been so altered
> by that celestial accident.

> Its atmosphere is laden now
> with fragrant memory,

its nights and days now pulse
with the ardent vigor of stars.

> Its winds now sing
> new harmonies,

> its waterways now flow
> toward reconfigured seas.

HALF MOON

This dilemma —
I try to tell about it
when friends ask how I am.
This being in love —
is it a problem to be solved?
A joy? A tragedy?
A riddle on the tongue of a fool?

I don't know.
But whatever it is
it reconfigures my day,
magnifies beauty,
intensifies light,
even alters the meaning of time.

But I've been fooled before.
There's reason for caution
even here under familiar stars.
Sometimes by the light
of the half-moon
shadows are cast
by even the surest knowing.

WHATEVER IT IS

How did Rumi do it?
  Would he tell me,
  even if he could?

He might say
  there is nothing
  to be said.

He might say
  try anyway.

He might say
  tell what you love
  that you love it,
  nothing more.

    One word too many
    and the wine
    goes sour.

Whatever it is
that ripens the grape
is what I'm trying to say.

EMPTY PAGE

I've been listening
but I haven't heard a poem
in this desert wind, not yet

and so my pencil rests,
the empty page lifts up
and blows away, gone . . .

Maybe somewhere west of here
that empty page will land
at someone's feet

and maybe it will
beckon in the way
a nascent poem can.

It could happen
just like that —
my not-speaking

becomes someone else's song.

LETTER FROM SEA LEVEL TO MY FAMILY

White noise bothers me
but strong wind does not
so I came north.
My leaving doesn't mean
I love you less.
In fact from here
I hear more clearly
what you try to say.

       Here the tide seems glad
       to have me to itself.
       With love like this
       does it even matter
       where I am or what I do?
       If I ever write a song
       I hope it sounds
       like rain.

EMILY'S POEMS

Were they her medicine
for keeping spells at bay?
So many myths, I can't be sure.
Biographers project themselves —
their long-dead subject pays.
I like to think she woke predawn
to calibrate her teeming brain
with robin song.

I think she did her best
to map the place that trembled
like Vesuvius at times —
her own volcanic mind.
How generous she was to use
what some would call infirmity
as an exploratory tool,
translating her discoveries
into verse like jewels.

NOTHING LEFT TO SELL

I used to keep shop, like my father before me,
selling functional objects designed to delight
and brighten a home — lamps and candlesticks
and myrtlewood bowls, vases and plates
and teapots from China and cups from Japan,
stoneware handmade by potters who lived
near the river where good clay was found.

Now I've retired, like my father did.
The shop still stands and so do I, but now
its doors are closed and the shelves are bare.
So, who am I, if not a merchant of earthly goods?
Can I learn another trade at this late stage
or is it time to give it all away and step into
the new terrain of nothing left to sell?

www.ingramcontent.com/pod-product-compliance
Lightning Source LLC
Chambersburg PA
CBHW022123040426
42450CB00006B/823

Shanti Arts

Nature · Art · Spirit

Please visit us on online
to browse our entire book catalog,
including additional poetry collections and fiction,
books on travel, nature, healing, art,
photography, and more.

www.shantiarts.com

ABOUT THE AUTHOR

Stacie Smith was born in Salem, Oregon, in 1945. A fourth generation Oregonian, she grew up in Eugene, in the Willamette Valley. She was a student of William Stafford at Lewis and Clark College in the mid-1960s. Her poems have been published in numerous journals and magazines. Her first book of poems, *Open Burning*, was self-published in 2016. *Meanwhile the Earth: Poems from Cougar Creek* was published by Shanti Arts in September 2018.

Smith was awarded a writer's residency at Playa Summer Lake, Oregon, in 2014. The following year she was granted a residency through Oregon State University's Spring Creek "Trillium Project" at Shotpouch Creek Cabin. Smith has been a visual artist for over fifty years. Her paintings, prints, and sculpture are in numerous private and public collections. In June 2018 Smith was invited to present her work — science-related poetry and art — to the Yachats Academy of Arts and Sciences.

WHO CARES IF THE WORLD ENDS?

Ask the mote of pollen
      riding on the golden air.
Ask the newborn spider
      with its silken parachute
      adrift and at the mercy
      of the great unknown.
Ask the grey cat sleeping
      on the crimson rug.
Ask the weaver
      at her loom.
Ask the boatman
      and the refugee.
Ask the moon
      and ask the peach.
Ask the river
      and the sea.
Ask yourself.
Ask me.

NEXT
— for my father

He's translucent now.
Age has frayed his coverings.
He sees things differently,
sees deeper than before
but maybe not as far.
He knows the door
to who knows where
will be the one
he opens next.

He feels a sweet nostalgia
for what might have been.
The daily news becomes
too much to bear.
Yesterday is dim.
Tomorrow is a word
that makes no sense.
He quietly rejoices as he
sheds his name.

THE LETTER

leaving the house
to buy a stamp
— epic journey!

along the way
daphne might slay me
crocus might rob me blind

but I don't mind.
    the letter in my hand
    says thanks for everything.

DONNA'S PROMPTS SERIES XIV

crying mountain/discourse/schooner/
wrangle/cymbal

CRYING MOUNTAIN

Li Po — when I say his name, Li Po —
I feel what he saw on his way
away from what most men know.
He always walked alone
is what I have gleaned
from the one thin book about his life.

A sannyasin, he avoided discourse,
the tavern and the wrangling therein,
the clanging cymbals,
the rush to board the schooners
heading out from the harbor
in search of new worlds.

His world was the grey path
winding up and up and up
toward the summit of Crying Mountain.
from there he could behold it all —
the tavern, the town, the sea —
all reasons for the mountain's many tears.

ONE FOR THE PREY

Another one gone today
taken by the hungry wolf
while the rest of the flock
huddles in fear.

I light three candles —
      one for the shepherd
      one for the predator
      one for the prey.

Rain has fallen hard for days.
Bridges are washed away
as the creek takes ragged bites
from its own muddy flanks.

I light more candles —
      one for the stranded
      one for the roiling creek
      one for any creature
      caught in Nature's teeth.